Women of the Word

30 Days of Faith Building

Volume 1

By Heather Reid

IngramSpark
Australia

Women of the
Word

Contents

Forward

I first met Heather & Brian Reid in 2019 when we were travelling around Australia in our caravan, and in 2020 my husband Garry and I were blessed to be invited to stay with them at their home for about a year. Though the world was going through an upheaval, we felt like we were living in a sanctuary with daily Christian fellowship. Heather and I formed a close bond as we shared our love for the Word, experiences in our lives, and our unique talents.

It was during this time together that I recognized Heather's depth of knowledge of the Word and that her journey was unlike anyone else I'd met. Her many experiences from childhood through to that very day, were peppered with praises to the Lord where He had provided, healed, restored, and protected both her and her family. Heather would call them her 'God stories', always retold in such a way that I hung on to her every word.

Heather was at the time (and still is) a gifted classroom teacher and I encouraged her to put Bible stories online for the children who were (at that time) being schooled at home. One day as we were sitting having a 'cuppa' (cup of tea) together Heather shared with me that she would love to help women, especially young mothers grow in their

Christian faith. We prayed together asking God to make a way for her to do this. 'Women of the Word' on Facebook was born and now has nearly 2000 members and is growing daily.

I wholeheartedly endorse Heather's first Women of the Word daily devotional and believe you will be encouraged as you read her daily insight from the Word of God and enjoy her 'God stories'.

Gloria Preston
Grace Faith Christian Discipleship

www.gfcd.org.au

Day 1

Good morning, my friend,

The children of Israel had returned to Judah to rebuild the city and its temple. They wept when they saw the ruins, and they wept when they heard God's law and realised just how far they had gone from the Lord and his word. They wept so long and hard that Nehemiah stopped them and told them to *"Do not mourn or weep....Do not grieve, for the joy of the LORD is your strength"* (Nehemiah 8:9-10). Many of us today are feeling just like the Children of Israel. We have wept and grieved so long that we are exhausted. We have struggled and just worn ourselves out trying to do things in our own strength. We may be looking at the ruins of something that has just not worked out.

Isaiah 61:1-3 (a prophecy that Jesus later quoted in reference to Himself) says, *"The Spirit of the Lord GOD is upon Me, Because the LORD has anointed Me To preach good tidings to the poor; He has sent Me to heal the broken-hearted, To proclaim liberty to the captives, And the opening of the prison to those who are bound; To proclaim the acceptable year of the LORD, And the day of vengeance of our God; To comfort all who mourn, To console those who mourn in Zion, To give them beauty for ashes, The oil of joy for mourning, The garment of praise for the spirit of heaviness; That they may be called trees of righteousness, The planting of the LORD, that He may be glorified"* (NKJV). Joy is a fruit of the spirit and doesn't come from your flesh. So how do we release it? We laugh! We sing! We dance! We praise and worship God. You may say, "But I don't feel like it!" Well, it isn't based on feelings! Just like every other area of our lives, we walk by faith.

In 2021, my daughter Rachel had planned a beautiful wedding for my granddaughter Charlotte, only to have to cancel it for the second time because of the Covid lockdowns. Both Rachel and Charlotte grieved at the loss of not only her special day but also the thousands of dollars it had cost, which could not be retrieved. Sadness had taken hold of them as they walked into the bedroom where Charlotte's beautiful gown was still hanging on the door. Feeling miserable, they both lay on their backs on the floor, eating the chocolates they had been boxing as wedding favours for the guests. Suddenly, they began to laugh. They laughed and laughed till tears rolled down their cheeks. Joy welled up from within them, and they felt so much better afterwards. The situation hadn't changed, but they had. Psalm 32:11 says, *"Be glad in the Lord and rejoice, you righteous; and shout for joy, all you upright in heart"* (NKJV). The word 'rejoice' in the original Hebrew text means to 'leap up and spin around'.[1] Put on some praise music and as you rejoice (clap, leap, shout, sing, praise, laugh, spin around, or dance), the joy of the Lord will be released in you. The devil knows that if he can steal your joy, he can steal your strength. Don't let him!

Charlotte was finally married in December 2022, and the Lord saw to it that it was a perfect wedding in every way.

The joy of the Lord is your strength.

Have a wonderful day.

[1] James Strong, *Strong's Exhaustive Concordance of the Bible*, Greek Dictionary, entry G1523.

Day 2

Good morning, my friend,

Have you been praying and believing for something, but the answer seems to have been a long time coming? Philippians 4:6-7 says, *"Do not be anxious about anything, but in every situation, by prayer and petition, with thanksgiving, present your requests to God. And the peace of God, which transcends all understanding, will guard your hearts and your minds in Christ Jesus"*.

Notice verse 6 says, but in everything, by prayer and supplication, WITH THANKSGIVING, present your requests to God. Thanksgiving will lead to peace. Just the act of being grateful for all the blessings the Lord has already given you will settle you, take your mind off your problem, and bring you peace.

I remember once I had really lost my peace because we desperately needed a new lounge suite (furniture for my lounge room) and couldn't afford to buy one at that time. I was grumbling and complaining to the Lord in my quiet time, that I had been believing for one for over a year and nothing had eventuated. Feeling frustrated and disappointed, I picked up my Bible, and it flopped open to Deuteronomy 28:47, where it said that the children of Israel failed to receive from God and suffered lack because they did not joyfully thank God for the abundance of all things. Well, after reading that scripture, I knew the Lord was speaking to my heart. I had been grumbling and complaining, so I quickly repented and began to thank God for everything I could think of. All day long, I walked around my home thanking and praising God for the things God had already blessed me with, and as I did, I clapped my hands. By the end of the day, I started feeling a genuine joy bubbling up inside me, and I began to laugh. I laughed, and laughed, and laughed. It got to the point where I didn't care if I never got a lounge suite; I was so thankful for the things that I already had. All that night, I kept waking myself up laughing, and I knew that something had shifted in the realm of the spirit. The next morning, about 8.30 a.m., a man from our church (who had never been to my home) rang me and asked, "Are you praying for a lounge suite? Because if you are, we have two, and the Lord has told us to give you one." I nearly leapt through the phone! Yesss!!! On arriving at his house, he showed me two lounge suites. I chose the older one, and it was perfect, as if God had handpicked it out for me. I felt so blessed, and I know that they would have been blessed as well, because you cannot outgive God.

God will move on our behalf when we are thankful and begin to praise Him. The Bible says in 1 Thessalonians 5:18, *"In every situation [no matter what the circumstances] be thankful and continually give thanks to God; for this is the will of God for you in Christ Jesus"* (AMP). It is difficult to stay anxious and stressed when you are thankful.

Develop an attitude of gratitude. Find things today to give thanks to the Lord for, and watch God change your circumstances. His peace will guard your heart and mind.

God is good! Have a wonderful day

Day 3

ood morning, my friend,

Isn't it good to know that each day is a new day and the Lord's blessings, and mercy are new every morning? You may have had a terrible day yesterday. Sometimes life is like that. But there is hope for today.

In Lamentations 3:23 it says, *"Because of the loving devotion of the Lord we are not consumed, for His mercies never fail. They are new every morning; great is Your faithfulness! 'The Lord is my portion,' says my soul, 'therefore I will hope in Him'"* (BSB). The Hebrew word for 'new' as used here is the word 'chadash' meaning 'fresh, a new thing, to rebuild'.[2] I like that. I can re-build.

God still has plan A for our lives, even when we mess it up. His plan for us was established even before the foundation of the earth. Ephesians 1:4 says, *"According as he hath chosen us in him before the foundation of the world, that we should be holy and without blame before him in love"* (KJV).

1 John 1:9 says, *"If we confess our sins, he is faithful and just to forgive us our sins, and to cleanse us from all unrighteousness"* (NKJV).

When we repent, He will just bring us back into alignment with his original plan for our lives. That is why Philippians 3:13 says, *"Brothers and sisters, I do not consider myself yet to have taken hold of it. But one thing I do: Forgetting what is behind and straining toward what is ahead"*. We move on in the grace of God for today, praise God.

One thing I do, before I go to sleep at night, is to pray and repent for anything I may have done during that day that I know has grieved the Holy Spirit; and if I have been upset with anyone, I also forgive them. Not only does it help me sleep better, but it gives me a fresh start to my new day. God has promised to never remember them again so why should I?

If you are beating yourself up over where you have missed it, repent, let go of your past mistakes, stop condemning yourself, and move on in what God has planned for you today.

Romans 8:1-2 says, *"Therefore, there is now no condemnation for those who are in Christ Jesus, because through Christ Jesus the law of the Spirit who gives life has set you free from the law of sin and death"*

That is good news!

Have a wonderful day my friend.

[2] *Strong's Concordance*, H2319 (*chadash*).

Day 4

ood morning, my friend,

Throughout this book, I will be using the term 'Word of God' a lot. Why? Because Jesus is the living Word of God.

John 1:1-3 says, *"In the beginning was the Word, and the Word was with God, and the Word was God. The same was in the beginning with God. All things were made by him; and without him was not anything made that was made"* (KJV).

John 1:14, *"The Word became flesh and made His dwelling among us. We have seen His glory, the glory of the one and only Son from the Father, full of grace and truth"*.

Revelation 19:13, *"And he was clothed with a robe dipped in blood: and his name is called The Word of God"* (NKJV). Jesus is the Word!

In the Old Testament, God revealed His Word to His prophets, which was then written down, whereas in the New Testament, the Word of God was revealed in a person, Jesus Christ. The writers of the New Testament wrote as the Holy Spirit inspired them, and that Word is as powerful today as if Jesus himself just spoke it. When we receive revelation from the Word of God, it changes from a logos (a written word) to a rhema – a revealed word, as God quickens to us a certain text, or it may come to us through the spoken words of another person. Wikipedia defines rhema as "a specific word from the Lord that applies it to us individually." It is that 'ah ha' moment when you are reading or hearing something, and it becomes alive to you, and it may even seem to 'jump out' of the page at you. I have had many occasions in my life where the Lord has spoken to me specifically through a verse of Scripture that has given me such peace and comfort and was exactly what I needed to hear at the time.

The word of God is also how I am corrected and trained in righteousness. 2 Timothy 3:16-17 says, *"All Scripture is God -breathed and is useful for teaching, rebuking, correcting and training in righteousness, so that the servant of God may be thoroughly equipped for every good work"*.

If we do not know the Word of God, we can be easily deceived and led astray because it provides us with a solid foundation of truth and is our check and balance by which we test everything we hear or read. It is quick, powerful and sharper than a two-edged sword. It is the Word of God that has the power to change our circumstances, and when we speak the word in faith, it is as powerful as if God were speaking it himself.

God exalts his Word and his Name above all else. *"I will worship toward thy holy temple, and praise thy name for thy lovingkindness and for thy truth: for thou hast magnified thy word above all thy name"* (Psalm 138, KJV). It pays to know God's Word.

Be blessed, my friend, and have a wonderful day.

Day 5

ood morning, my friend,

I want to share with you one of the most important lessons I have ever learned in my walk with the Lord, and that is to forgive others quickly and not hold a grudge. Ephesians 4:31-32 says, *"Let all bitterness, and wrath, and anger, and clamour, and evil speaking, be put away from you, with all malice: And be ye kind one to another, tender-hearted, forgiving one another, even as God for Christ's sake hath forgiven you"* (KJV).

You may say – "Yeah, but you do not know what happened to me or what that person said or did to me. It was so bad that I just cannot forgive them."

Jesus told a story to illustrate why we must forgive. *"Therefore is the kingdom of heaven likened unto a certain king, which would take account of his servants. And when he had begun to reckon, one was brought unto him, which owed him ten thousand talents. But forasmuch as he had not to pay, his lord commanded him to be sold, and his wife, and children, and all that he had, and payment to be made. The servant therefore fell down, and worshipped him, saying, Lord, have patience with me, and I will pay thee all. Then the lord of that servant was moved with compassion, and loosed him, and forgave him the debt. But the same servant went out, and found one of his fellow-servants, which owed him a hundred pence: and he laid hands on him, and took him by the throat, saying, Pay me what you owe me. And his fellow-servant fell down at his feet, and besought him, saying, have patience with me, and I will pay you all. And he would not: but went and cast him into prison, till he should pay the debt. So, when his fellow servants saw what was done, they were very sorry, and came and told unto their lord all that was done. Then his lord, after he had called him, said unto him, O you wicked servant, I forgave you all that debt, because you asked me: Why didn't you also have had compassion on your fellow-servant, even as I had pity on you? And his lord was very angry, and delivered him to the tormentors, till he should pay all that was due unto him. So likewise, shall my heavenly Father do also unto you, if you from your hearts don't forgive your brother their trespasses"* (Matthew 18:28-35, KJV).

That story is a perfect example of what God has done for us. He has completely wiped our debt and forgiven us our sins. He wants us to forgive others the same way he has forgiven us. When we hold a grudge against someone, we are hurting ourselves, and in a strange way, we allow that person to continue to control us. We also give the devil legal right to torment us. Forgiveness does not mean you are condoning what that person has done to you. Forgiveness is extending to the person who hurt you, mercy, even though they don't deserve it. In the natural, you will not be able to forgive, but with the supernatural power of God's love, you can forgive, you can let go and walk on.

Be blessed and have a wonderful day.

Day 6

ood morning, my friend,

Philippians 3:13-14 says, *"Brethren, I count not myself to have apprehended: but this one thing I do, forgetting those things which are behind, and reaching forth unto those things which are before, I press toward the mark for the prize of the high calling of God in Christ Jesus"* (KJV).

Have you ever seen a race where one of the runners keeps looking back to see where the others are? You will notice that the more he looks back, the slower he goes and the more likely he is to stumble. It is the same with us. If we keep looking back, then we won't see where we are going. God wants to encourage you today to let go of the past and move forward in his marvellous plan for your life, keeping your eyes firmly fixed on Jesus.

2 Corinthians 5:17 says, *"Therefore if any man be in Christ, he is a new creature: old things are passed away; behold, all things are become new"* (KJV). Isn't that amazing! When you give your life to the Lord Jesus Christ, he gives you a brand-new spirit, a completely new creation. The old person you were passed away. You are not the same person anymore, so do not look back! Your old life has gone. Jesus dealt with it at the cross.

I remember reading a story about a preacher who had lived a pretty bad life before he got saved, but when a man asked him about his past, he told him, "That man you are talking about has died. I am a new creation in Christ Jesus." I like that because it is true. You have been reborn to a new life in Christ Jesus.

Isaiah 43:18 says, *"Do not call to mind the former things; pay no attention to the things of old"* (BSB). The devil loves to come along and torment you with your past. Romans 8:1 says, *"There is therefore now no condemnation to them which are in Christ Jesus, who walk not after the flesh, but after the Spirit"* (NKJV). Hebrews 10:17 says that God will remember your sins and lawless deeds NO MORE. So, tell the devil to leave in Jesus name! DO NOT LOOK BACK! Press on to the higher things God has called you to. You have a job to do!

Have a wonderful day, my friend.

Day 7

Good morning, my friend,

Did you know that your thoughts have a profound effect on every part of your body? Research done by Dr Caroline Leaf has also found that our negative thoughts can also be the root cause of many of our physical problems. The Word of God also tells us that what we think is very important.

Proverbs 23:7 says, *"For as he thinks in his heart, so is he"* (NKJV).

Philippians 4:6-7 says, *"Do not fret or have any anxiety about anything, but in every circumstance and in everything, by prayer and petition (definite requests), with thanksgiving, continue to make your wants known to God. And God's peace [shall be yours, that tranquil state of a soul assured of its salvation through Christ, and so fearing nothing from God and being content with its earthly lot of whatever sort that is, that peace] which transcends all understanding shall garrison and mount guard over your hearts and minds in Christ Jesus"* (AMP).

Ephesians 4:22 says, *"That ye put off concerning the former conversation the old man, which is corrupt according to the deceitful lusts; And be renewed in the spirit of your mind"* (KJV). It simply means – meditate on God's Word. Fill your mind with what God says, and as you do, you will change your thoughts to line up with His thoughts.

2 Corinthians 10:4-5 says, *"The weapons we fight with are not the weapons of the world. On the contrary, they have divine power to demolish strongholds. We demolish arguments and every pretension that sets itself up against the knowledge of God, and we take captive every thought to make it obedient to Christ"*.

The original Greek for the word mighty says, 'they have divine Power' and that word is – dunamai – and is where we get the word dynamite.

The way to deal with negative thoughts is to take those thoughts captive and bring them to Jesus. I have found this to be an incredibly powerful way to deal with thoughts that start raging in my mind. I just say out loud, "I cast that thought down in the mighty name of Jesus! I demolish your stronghold in my mind. I take you captive, and I bring you to Jesus Christ."

Philippians 4:8 says, *"Finally, brethren, whatever things are true, whatever things are noble, whatever things are just, whatever things are pure, whatever things are lovely, whatever things are of good report, if there is any virtue and if there is anything praiseworthy—meditate on these things"* (NKJV). It is time for us to replace the bad thoughts with the word of God. It will renew your mind and give you peace.

Be blessed, my dear friend, and have a wonderful day.

Day 8

Good morning, my friend,

Proverbs 4:7 says, *"Wisdom is the principal thing; therefore get wisdom: and with all thy getting get understanding"* (KJV).

I am sure that life would be so much better if everyone had wisdom. Can you imagine the mistakes (some costly) that we could have avoided had we listened to wisdom? The Bible says that wisdom is the principal or supreme thing, and it is available to everyone.

James 1:5-6 says, *"If any of you lacks wisdom, let him ask of God, who gives to all liberally and without reproach, and it will be given to him"* (NKJV).

I remember when I was first married, I prayed earnestly that the Lord would give me wisdom, but then I wondered how I would know that I had received it. I asked the Lord to give me a scripture on this, and when I opened my daily reading that day from a little book called Daily Light, it said, *"Happy is the man that finds wisdom, and the man that gets understanding"* (Prov 3:13). I figured the Lord had heard my prayer and I had received it.

Now whenever I need wisdom and understanding, especially when I am reading God's word or making big decisions, I always ask for it because God has promised to give it. All you must do is receive it by faith and believe you have it.

Solomon prayed for wisdom and understanding and wrote the

book of Proverbs. He said in Proverbs 3:13-18,

> *"Blessed is the man who finds wisdom,*
> *the man who acquires understanding,*
> *for she is more profitable than silver,*
> *and her gain is better than fine gold.*
> *She is more precious than rubies;*
> *nothing you desire compares with her.*
> *Long life is in her right hand;*
> *in her left hand are riches and honour.*
> *All her ways are pleasant,*
> *and all her paths are peaceful.*
> *She is a tree of life to those who embrace her,*
> *and those who lay hold of her are blessed* (BSB).

If you get wisdom, you get everything.

Blessings on you, my friend. Have a wonderful day.

Day 9

ood morning, my friend,

James 5:16-18 says, *"Therefore, confess your sins to each other and pray for each other so that you may be healed. The prayer of a righteous person is powerful and effective. Elijah was a human being, even as we are. He prayed earnestly that it would not rain, and it did not rain on the land for three and a half years. Again he prayed, and the heavens gave rain, and the earth produced its crops"*.

Would you like your prayers to be powerful and effective? The first thing to understand is that you are righteous. Righteous is a word that we don't use much these days. It is a legal term, and it simply means the state of being morally correct, just, upright, and having right standing with God. Most of us would pull the pin right there and say, "Oh, well, that disqualifies me then, so how will I ever get my prayers answered?" Here is the good news - 2 Corinthians 5:21 says, *"God made Him who knew no sin to be sin on our behalf, so that in Him we might become the righteousness of God"*.

When you accepted Jesus as your Saviour, he took your sins, all of them - past, present, future, plus all the ordinances (or accusations) against you and nailed them to his cross when he died. He gave you the gift of salvation, his own righteousness, blotted out your sins and no longer holds them against you. So, if you do the wrong thing and sin, you can go to the Father, repent, and say sorry (1 John 1:9), and Jesus becomes your Advocate and pleads your innocence because of what has already been done for you at the cross.

Hebrews 10:14 says, *"For by one sacrifice he has made perfect forever those who are being made holy"*.

Wow! That means that when you go to him in prayer, you do not have to feel unworthy or condemned. He has opened the way for you to go before your Heavenly Father – as if you had never sinned! It is not based on your righteousness, but on His righteousness. Now you can approach God with confidence, knowing that he hears you when you pray. That is good news!

I remember for years if I did something wrong and my conscience accused me of it, I would go for days and days without praying or reading my bible, just because I thought that God was angry with me. I felt condemned, and it affected my wanting to fellowship with Him. Then one day, I read the verse above in Hebrews 10:14, and it totally set me free. It was all done at the cross 2000 years ago! The sacrifice Jesus made was so complete that there is nothing more to be done. My sins were dealt with – past, present, and future and now God sees me as perfect. Just knowing that gives me confidence to enter His presence, as if I had never sinned. Isn't that awesome?

Be blessed, my friend. Have a wonderful day!

Day 10

ood morning, my friend,

Do you want to know how to pray in line with the will of God? We often hear the prayer prayed, "Lord, if it be thy will," especially regarding healing, but do you know that you can pray with absolute certainty if you already know what the will of God is?

1 John 5:14-15 says, *"And this is the confidence that we have before Him: If we ask anything according to His will, He hears us. And if we know that He hears us in whatever we ask, we know that we already possess what we have asked of Him. ..."* (BSB).

Wow! So, if I am reading correctly, John is saying here that once we have established what God's will is and pray in line with His will, then not only does he hear us, but it is already granted to us. So, how do we determine what the will of God is? We look at Jesus.

Jesus came to DO the will of his Father (Matthew 11:2-6). He was God's will in action! Everything He did was the will of his Father. *"So Jesus replied, 'Truly, truly, I tell you, the Son can do nothing by Himself, unless He sees the Father doing it. For whatever the Father does, the Son also does'"* (John 5:19, BSB).

So, looking at Jesus, we know straight away that it is his will to heal the sick. Matthew 15:30 says, *"Great crowds came to him, bringing the lame, the blind, the crippled, the mute and many others, and laid them at his feet; and he healed them."*

Everywhere Jesus went, He healed the sick, and not only that, He commissioned his disciples to do the same.

Jesus has already provided healing for you at the cross. Isaiah 53:4-5 says, *"Surely he took up our pain and bore our suffering, yet we considered him punished by God, stricken by him, and afflicted. But he was pierced for our transgressions, he was crushed for our iniquities; the punishment that brought us peace was on him, and by his wounds we are healed"*.

Young's Literal Translation writes it like this, *"Surely our sicknesses he hath borne, and our pains -- he hath carried them, And we -- we have esteemed him plagued, Smitten of God, and afflicted."*[3] This passage is made very clear by Matthew, where he speaks of the same passage of Scripture and uses the words, *'bore our infirmities and carried our sicknesses'* (Matthew 8:17).

The Lord wants you well! All you have to do is receive your healing like a little child, then believe it is done and thank him.

Have a wonderful day, my friend.

---

[3] Robert Young, *Young's Literal Translation of the Holy Bible*.

Day 11

Good morning, my friend,

I remember when my children were still at home, we decided, along with another family of 6, to head north to see the wildflowers. It was in the Spring season, and we had told the kids about the carpets of flowers they would see along the way, so it was all very exciting. It was also a very spontaneous decision, as we had decided to just pack up our cars and head off for the weekend. We thought we would go up through the middle of Western Australia to Mt Magnet, a country town, and maybe stay at the hotel there before heading home. I rang the Hotel and yes, they had a vacancy for all of us. When we arrived at Mt. Magnet, the hotel was not up to standard, so we decided to continue driving to Geraldton, but by the time we got there, it was getting dark, and we needed a hotel to accommodate us all. Every hotel had signs, "Full up" because there was a motocross event happening in town, so we decided to keep on driving to Kalbarri, further north on the coast, but this time thought we would ring ahead. As I rang, I prayed fervently, asking the Lord for a miracle because we had children with us who were very tired, and I believed that God would supply all our needs and provide a place for us. When I contacted the first place, the lady said, "We are totally booked out because we have a major event going on up here too, but I will ring around for you." While I waited, I kept thanking God for our miracle. When I rang her back, she said with a surprised sound in her voice, "There were no vacancies anywhere, but do you know what just happened? I had a call from someone cancelling two family suites. They are yours if you want them." We ended up in Kalbarri and had a wonderful time there. God is good!

Did you know that without faith it is impossible to please God? (Hebrews 11:6) The verse goes on to say that anyone who comes to Him must believe that He exists and that He rewards those who earnestly seek Him. As you can see, faith is very important to God, and in 1 John 5:4 it says, *"For whatever is born of God overcomes the world. And this is the victory that has overcome the world— our faith"* (NKJV). Our spirit has been born of God, so this passage is talking about us!

Hebrews 11:1 tells us, *"Now faith is the substance of things hoped for, the evidence of things not seen"* (KJV). Faith has substance, or as the original text says, it is the assurance and is like our Title Deed. I own a block down by the water in Australind, Western Australia. It has been paid for, and I have the title deed, and even if I were overseas, that block is still mine because I have a bit of paper that says it is. Well, we have a Bible full of promises, and we own those promises because the body and blood of our Lord Jesus Christ has paid for them. "For no matter how many promises God has made, they are 'Yes' in Christ. And so through him the "Amen" is spoken by us to the glory of God" (2 Corinthians 1:20). He is not saying "No" to us, He is saying "YES!" When we receive those promises from God's Word, our faith is our Title Deed! Then whenever the devil comes to tell us that we don't have them, we simply speak God's word in faith and say, "Yes I do devil, God's word says…I believe it and that settles it!"

It is not trying to conjure up faith, or work at faith, it is simply believing that what God has said is true, receiving it like a little child, and thanking Him for it even though you can't see it yet. That is the faith that pleases God!

Be blessed my friend, have a wonderful day.

Day 12

ood morning, my friend,

Hebrews 11:6 says, *"But without faith it is impossible to please Him, for he who comes to God must believe that He is, and that He is a rewarder of those who diligently seek Him"* (NKJV).

So, what is faith? The dictionary defines faith as 'Complete trust or confidence in someone or something.'

The Bible defines faith in Hebrews 11:1, *"Now faith is confidence in what we hope for and assurance about what we do not see"*. It is how we start our journey with the Lord. We put our faith in God's grace to save us, and we believe in and receive Jesus Christ as our Lord and Saviour. We believe the Word of God to be the truth. We believe that ALL the promises of God are "yes, in Christ, and Amen."

I remember a time when Brian and I were as poor as Church mice, having left our jobs to work for a Church that was in its infancy. Our income just supplied our needs, not our wants, so we had to believe for everything else. On Sundays, it was a tradition in the Church we attended for everyone to go out to lunch after Church and even though we desired to go, we just could not afford the luxury. On the way to Church, Joshua (our five-year-old) asked us whether we could go out for pizza after Church had finished and I started to say "Sorry son but we can't afford it" when the Lord stopped me, so I said to him "Josh, God is our provider, if you can believe for the money, then we will go for pizza". In his childlike way, he prayed and asked the Lord to supply that need. After Church had finished a lady who had never been to our Church before, came across from the other side of the church and with a measure of embarrassment said, "Look, I have waited till the last because I was not sure if I heard God or not, but here is some money. I heard the Lord say during the service that I was to give it to you." She brought her hand from behind her back and handed me a small wad of notes. It was with great joy that I accepted it and told her then how we had prayed on the way to Church and that God had used her to answer our prayer. When I looked at the amount, it was enough for the 'All you can eat' pizza at Pizza Hut. She left so encouraged, knowing she had heard God, and we left with great joy, heading for the Pizza Hut. Praise the Lord! A little boy learned that God does hear and answer prayer, and that God is a rewarder of those who diligently seek Him! So today, be like little Joshua, take God at His word and believe.

Be blessed my friend, and have a wonderful day.

Day 13

Good morning, my friend,

Jesus said in John 14:27, *"Peace I leave with you, my peace I give to you; not as the world gives do I give to you. Let not your heart be troubled, neither let it be afraid"* (NKJV). Isn't it incredible that we can have the same peace that Jesus had? Was he afraid of the storm at sea, no! He calmed the storm. Was he afraid of catching a disease from the people thronging him? No! He healed the diseases. Was he afraid of having no food? No! He used a boy's lunch to feed the multitude. Was he afraid when the devil came to test him? No! He gave him the Word of God! Jesus knew who he was, and he knew what he had. So why are we so afraid when we have been given the same peace?

Philippians 4:6-7 says, *"Do not be anxious about anything, but in every situation, by prayer and petition, with thanksgiving, present your requests to God. And the peace of God, which transcends all understanding, will guard your hearts and your minds in Christ Jesus"* (NKJV).

When trouble comes, as it does to all of us, don't lose your peace. *"Cast all your anxiety on him because he cares for you"*. The word 'cast' in the original Greek means 'to hurl', and one of the ways I deal with my problems and anxieties is to hold my hands out in front of me and then imagine placing all my worries into my hands. When I have done that, I pray, "Father, these are my worries, anxieties and cares. They are too big for me to handle and are robbing me of my peace, so right now I am casting them up to you like you said to do. In Jesus name." I then hurl those cares right up to Him to take care of and leave them with Him. You will find it is very cathartic to do so. Now, when you give your cares to God, make sure that you don't take them back. As you leave them with Him, believe that He is sorting them out for you, trust Him to take care of it all and begin to thank Him for the answers.

John 14:27, *"Peace I leave with you, My peace I give to you; not as the world gives do I give to you. Let not your heart be troubled, neither let it be afraid"* (NKJV).

Isaiah 26:3: *"You will keep him in perfect peace, whose mind is stayed on You, because he trusts in You"* (NKJV).

God bless you, my friend. Have a wonderful day.

Day 14

Good morning, my friend,

Philippians 2:9 says, *"Therefore God exalted Him to the highest place and gave Him the name above all names, that at the name of Jesus every knee should bow, in heaven and on earth and under the earth, and every tongue confess that Jesus Christ is Lord, to the glory of God the Father"* (BSB). Acts 4:12 says, *"Salvation is found in no one else, for there is no other name under heaven given to mankind by which we must be saved"*. There is power in that name!

Jesus has given us His name to use; in fact, He said, *"And whatever you might ask in My name, this I will do, so that the Father may be glorified in the Son"* (John 14:13).

"In that day you will no longer ask me anything. Very truly I tell you, my Father will give you whatever you ask in my name. Until now you have not asked for anything in my name. Ask and you will receive, and your joy will be complete." (John 16:23-24). A well-known writer, E.W. Kenyon, wrote, *"It is like we have been given power of Attorney to use His Name."* That is amazing!

Acts 3:6-16, *"Then Peter said, 'Silver and gold I do not have, but what I do have I give you: In the name of Jesus Christ of Nazareth, rise up and walk.' And he took him by the right hand and lifted him up, and immediately his feet and ankle bones received strength……Now, as the lame man who was healed held on to Peter and John, all the people ran together to them in the porch, which is called Solomon's, greatly amazed. So when Peter saw it, he responded to the people: 'Men of Israel, why do you marvel at this? Or why look so intently at us, as though by our own power or godliness we had made this man walk? The God of Abraham, Isaac, and Jacob, the God of our fathers, glorified His Servant Jesus, whom you delivered up and denied in the presence of Pilate, when he was determined to let Him go. But you denied the Holy One and the Just, and asked for a murderer to be granted to you, and killed the Prince of life, whom God raised from the dead, of which we are witnesses. And His name, through faith in His name, has made this man strong, whom you see and know. Yes, the faith which comes through Him has given him this perfect soundness in the presence of you all'"* (NKJV). Jesus wants us to do the same works that he did, and greater – IN HIS NAME! (John 14:12-14).

Mark 16-18 says, *"Whoever believes and is baptised will be saved, but whoever does not believe will be condemned. And these signs will accompany those who believe: In my name they will drive out demons; they will speak in new tongues; they will pick up snakes with their hands; and when they drink deadly poison, it will not hurt them at all; they will place their hands on sick people, and they will get well"*.

Praise God for the wonderful Name of Jesus!

You are very blessed, my friend. Have a wonderful day.

Day 15

Good morning, my friend,

We have all been given the measure of faith, and we have found out that we do not need a lot of faith to move a mountain - only a mustard seed-sized faith, so why is it that we find ourselves floundering, lacking confidence, full of doubt and fear? Peter found himself in the same situation. He began to walk on the water towards Jesus, but as soon as he saw the strength of the wind, he was afraid, began to sink, and called for help. *"Immediately, Jesus reached out his hand and caught him. 'O you of little faith, why did you doubt?'"* (Matthew 14:31, NKJV). So, what was it that caused Peter to doubt and lose confidence? Verse 30 tells us. It says that he saw the strength of the wind. How did he see that? He took his eyes off Jesus and started looking at the problem!

"Now it happened, on a certain day, that He got into a boat with His disciples. And He said to them, 'Let us cross over to the other side of the lake'" (Luke 8:22, NKJV). That word by itself should have been enough, but again, when the wind grew boisterous, the disciples feared for their lives. Jesus was so confident that what he had said would come to pass, he was sleeping in the front of the boat. When the disciples woke him up, shouting, "Master, master, we perish!" He got up, rebuked the storm, and the sea became calm again. Then He said to them, "Where is your faith?" He didn't say they didn't have any faith. He just wanted to know why they were not using their faith. He wanted them to show him their faith by their

actions, which in this case, would have been to speak to that storm.

We read of little faith and great faith in the stories Jesus told. The Centurion (Matthew 8:10) and the Syrophoenician woman (Matthew 15:28) both had great faith. So, what was the difference in their faith and the faith the disciples had on the Sea of Galilee? The difference was that the Centurion and the Syrophoenician woman did not require evidence to believe. They departed from Jesus, believing in His word alone. That is great faith!

Jesus is the same yesterday, today and forever! What he did in biblical times, he is still doing today! So, if you are in a bad situation, go to God's Word, find a promise that you can believe, receive it by faith, and then stand firm on that promise by thanking God for it every day. Keep your eyes on Jesus and don't look at the problem! Trust that what God has said, he will do. That, my friend, is strong faith!

Be blessed and have a wonderful day!

Day 16

ood morning, my friend,

Did you know that one of the quickest ways to negate your own prayer for something is to allow doubt and unbelief to use your own tongue against you? It says in James 1:6-8, *"But when you ask, you must believe and not doubt, because the one who doubts is like a wave of the sea, blown and tossed by the wind. That person should not expect to receive anything from the Lord. Such a person is double-minded and unstable in all they do"*.

God's Word also says in Proverbs 18:21, *"Death and life are in the power of the tongue, and those who love it and indulge it will eat its fruit and bear the consequences of their words"* (AMP).

Our tongue has great power to produce good things, or bad things (fruit) in our life and like Proverbs says, we will eat its fruit! While we are double-minded, we will receive nothing from God! We must be single-minded about believing God's word, and if we do a check-up and find that we are being double minded then do as it says in 2 Corinthians 10:5, *"Casting down imaginations, and every high thing that exalts itself against the knowledge of God, and bringing into captivity every thought to the obedience of Christ"* (KJV). Take hold of those thoughts of fear. Do not let doubt and unbelief speak to you! Cast those thoughts down, speak only God's word and do not allow yourself to move from that position of faith. Faith and patience inherit the promises.

Matthew 15:11:

"What goes into someone's mouth does not defile them, but what comes out of their mouth, that is what defiles them."

Proverbs 21:23:

"Those who guard their mouths and their tongues keep themselves from calamity."

Proverbs 6:2:

"You have been trapped by what you said, ensnared by the words of your mouth."

Matthew 12:36:

"But I tell you that men will give an account on the day of judgement for every careless word they have spoken" (BSB).

God wants us to be careful with our words because words have creative power both for good and bad. When we speak God's word, He watches over it to perform it (Jeremiah 1:12).

God bless you, my friend. Have a wonderful day.

Day 17

Good morning, my friend,

Colossians 2:6 says, *"So then, just as you received Christ Jesus as Lord, continue to live your lives in him."* 1 John 2:6 goes on to say, *"Whoever claims to live in him must live as Jesus did."* So here we get the picture that as believers, our walk must be a daily walk – in union with Him, our lives representing Him as if He were here. That word 'walk' is from the Greek word 'peri' and 'pateo'; meaning to tread all around, i.e. walk at large; figuratively, to live, deport oneself, follow.[4] Christians should be a living example of the Lord Jesus Christ on this earth. We are an extension of Him, and we represent Him to this world.

How are we to do this? By looking into His Word. Colossians 3:10 says, *"And have put on the new man, which is renewed in knowledge after the image of him that created him"* (NKJV). As we look at God's Word, it is like a mirror. We can see who God says we are, and we are changed daily into His image. *"And we all, who with unveiled faces contemplate the Lord's glory, are being transformed into his image with ever-increasing glory, which comes from the Lord, who is the Spirit"* (2 Corinthians 3:18). *"For those God foreknew he also predestined to be conformed to the image of his Son, that he might be the firstborn among many brothers and sisters"* (Romans 8:29).

Ephesians 5:1-33 says, *"Be ye therefore followers of God, as dear children.."* (KJV). Another translation says, *"Be imitators of God"* (NKJV).

1 Corinthians 6:17 says, *"But he that is joined unto the Lord is one spirit.."* (KJV).

As we walk in close union with Him and as we live as He lived, everyone around us should see Jesus in us. We won't have to try because it will be evident in us, an outflowing of the river of life from within us.

You are blessed. Have a wonderful day.

---

[4] *Strong's Concordance*, G4043 (*peripateō*).

Day 18

Good morning, my friend,

Proverbs 23:7 says, *"For as he thinks in his heart, so is he. "Eat and drink!" he says to you, but his heart is not with you"* (NKJV).

This verse, in its context, refers to a man saying something but not really meaning it. In other words, he is a hypocrite. He may be saying all the right things, but inside, he does not believe what he is saying; his heart believes something else. This can often be our problem when standing on the Word of God for whatever we are believing for. I may be saying all the right things, but am I really believing it with my heart? God is not stupid. He sees our heart. The Lord pointed this out to me one day when I was speaking the Word of God about a situation I was in, and yet I was being a hypocrite because I really didn't believe what I was saying. I was just mouthing words without faith.

Hebrews 4:1-3 talks about this, *"Let us therefore fear, lest a promise being left us of entering into his rest, any of you should seem to come short of it. For unto us was the gospel preached, as well as unto them: but the word preached did not profit them, not being mixed with faith in them that heard it"* (NKJV). So, you see, when we find a promise in God's Word that quickens in our spirit, then we need to mix our faith with it, thanking God till we see it come to pass in our lives.

Many years ago, I had severe tachycardia to the point where I would have to lie flat on the floor to get my heart to clunk back into its correct rhythm, and on one occasion, I even ended up in Emergency because of a severe attack. The doctor talked of putting a pacemaker in my heart to deal with it, so I desperately went to the Word of God for an answer, looking for something that would come alive to me and was a rhema (a quickened word) to my heart. Psalm 112:7 said, *"He shall not be afraid of evil tidings: his heart is fixed, trusting in the LORD"* (NKJV). The Holy Spirit quickened it to me, and that was my verse, the one I could believe, so every day I would say, "Thank you Father, my heart is fixed, I am trusting in You!" I must have said that verse hundreds of times, especially if I felt my heartbeat was on the verge of being irregular, but I really believed that it was my promise from God, and it gave me peace. Sometime during those months, the Tachycardia completely disappeared and never came back. I was completely healed. That was some 30 years ago now. There is incredible power in the Word of God – if you mix faith with it, glory to God!

Bless you my friend, have a wonderful day.

Day 19

Good morning, my friend,

Faith and fear are opposites. If you are in fear, then you are no longer in faith, and we know that without faith it is impossible to please God. Faith is having confidence that what God has said, he will do.

David the Psalmist knew what it was to feel fear. He was right in the middle of a great battle with the Philistines when he wrote Psalm 56:3, *"My enemies would daily swallow me up: for they are many that fight against me, O thou most high. Whenever I am afraid, I will trust in you. In God I will praise his word, in God I have put my trust; I will not fear what flesh can do unto me"* (KJV). David knew how to encourage himself in the Lord. He spoke God's word and reminded himself of just how powerful God is. So here are some scriptures to encourage yourself with:

Psalm 118:6-7

"The Lord is with me; I will not be afraid. What can man do to me? The Lord is with me; he is my helper."

2 Timothy 1:7

"For God has not given us a spirit of fear, but of power and of love and of a sound mind."

Psalm 34:4

"I prayed to the Lord, and he answered me. He freed me from all my fears."

Philippians 4:6-7

"Do not be anxious about anything, but in every situation, by prayer and petition, with thanksgiving, present your requests to God. And the peace of God, which transcends all understanding, will guard your hearts and your minds in Christ Jesus."

John 14:27

"Peace is what I leave with you; it is my own peace that I give you. I do not give it as the world does. Do not be worried and upset; do not be afraid."

Matthew 6:34

"Therefore, do not worry about tomorrow, for tomorrow will worry about itself. Each day has enough trouble of its own."

God is on your side, my friend. Speak to fear and tell it to go. Cast all your cares on the Lord and encourage yourself with His word. He cares for you more than you know.

Be blessed and have a wonderful day, my friend.

Day 20

ood morning, my friend,

Have you ever felt confused and stressed to the point of despair because you don't know what to do? Well, the Children of Israel were in the same position. They were afraid because of some situation in their lives and were turning in circles trying to figure out what they should do. Some were saying, why don't we just pack up all our belongings on our horses and head back to Egypt. Pharaoh will be able to save us if we bargain with him. Well, God had something to say about that. He sent Isaiah to them with a message and said, "Woe to those who go down to Egypt for help, who rely on horses, who trust in the multitude of their chariots and in the great strength of their horsemen, but do not look to the Holy One of Israel, or seek help from the Lord." They were in confusion and fear because they had been putting their trust in man rather than trusting in the Lord.

Just recently, I had to cast a situation onto the Lord and leave it with Him. It was the hardest thing I have had to do. I wanted to sort out my situation by myself, but couldn't get a resolution to my problem, and it was causing me many sleepless nights. Finally, I cast it up to the Lord and told him that I was completely trusting Him with the situation and went to sleep like a baby. Within two days, He had supernaturally sorted it out for me. Isaiah 26:3 says, *"You will keep him in perfect peace whose mind is stayed on You, because he trusts in You."* The Hebrew meaning of peace is שָׁלוֹם (šā·lō·wm) -: Safe, well, happy, friendly, welfare, health, prosperity, peace.[5] Remember the word 'Shalom?' It has the same meaning. The Hebrew word for 'perfect' is the same Hebrew word שָׁלוֹם (šā·lō·wm) as used for 'peace.' That means a double amount of safety, welfare, health, prosperity, and peace is due to you when you trust in God and keep your mind stayed on Him.

Philippians 4:6-7,

"Do not be anxious about anything, but in every situation, by prayer and petition, with thanksgiving, present your requests to God. And the peace of God, which transcends all understanding, will guard your hearts and your minds in Christ Jesus."

God wants you stay in peace my friend so keep your mind stayed on Him.

Be blessed and have a wonderful day.

---

[5] *Strong's Concordance*, H7965 (*shalom*).

Day 21

Good morning, my friend,

It is so easy to get so busy doing 'stuff' for God that we do not spend any time with him. It would be like a marriage where one partner is never home. The devil knows that if he can distract us and get us so busy that we don't spend time with our Heavenly Father, he can rob us blind. Psalm 91 is conditional upon our abiding in the Secret Place under his wings. I believe that when we take the time each day to spend with the Lord, even a short amount of time, we will see the benefits in our health, our relationships, and every other area of our lives. So, find a place where you won't be interrupted, and spend some time with Him. Meditate on His Word and talk with Him about your day. He is the friend who sticks closer than a brother, and most of all, He desires a relationship.

Psalm 37:7

"I will sit before the Lord and wait patiently for him."

Isaiah 30:15

"In quietness and confidence will be your strength."

Psalm 23:1-3

"The Lord is my Shepherd; I lack nothing. He makes me lie down in green pastures, he leads me beside quiet waters, he refreshes my soul."

Isaiah 40:31

"But those who wait on the Lord Shall renew their strength;

They shall mount up with wings like eagles They shall run and not be weary, They shall walk and not faint."

Psalm 91:1-2

"He who dwells in the secret place of the Most High will abide in the shadow of the Almighty. I will say of the Lord, 'You are my refuge and my fortress, my God, in whom I trust.'"

The Lord is waiting to speak to you, so find a place where you can get quiet enough to listen to what He has to say. He wants a relationship with you.

You are blessed, my friend. Have a wonderful day.

Day 22

ood morning, my friend,

Did you know that most things we worry about never come to pass? It's true! We waste so much energy on worrying that we stop enjoying life. The bible has a lot to say about worrying. You see worry is just another form of fear, and fear and faith are opposites. When we worry, we are telling God that we do not believe that He is able to take care of us, whereas when we humble ourselves and commit everything to the Lord, we can then rest in His promises, protection and love and watch Him do what we can't do.

Do Not Worry

"Therefore, I tell you, do not worry about your life, what you will eat or drink; or about your body, what you will wear. Is not life more than food, and the body more than clothes? Look at the birds of the air: They do not sow or reap or gather into barns—and yet your heavenly Father feeds them. Are you not much more valuable than they? Who of you by worrying can add a single hour to his life.

And why do you worry about clothes? Consider how the lilies of the field grow: They do not labour or spin. Yet I tell you that not even Solomon in all his glory was adorned like one of these. If that is how God clothes the grass of the field, which is here today and tomorrow is thrown into the furnace, will He not much more clothe you, O you of little faith?

Therefore, do not worry, saying, 'What shall we eat?' or 'What shall we drink?' or 'What shall we wear?' For the Gentiles strive after all these things, and your heavenly Father knows that you need them. But seek first the kingdom of God and His righteousness, and all these things will be added unto you.

Therefore, do not worry about tomorrow, for tomorrow will worry about itself. Today has enough trouble of its own" (Matthew 6:25-34).

Philippians 4:6, *"Do not be anxious about anything, but in every situation, by prayer and petition, with thanksgiving, present your requests to God. And the peace of God, which transcends all understanding, will guard your hearts and your minds in Christ Jesus."*

Do not worry and have a wonderful day, my friend.

Day 23

Good morning, my friend,

Since the Covid Pandemic, everyone has become very conscious of cleanliness, with hand sanitizers on tables before you enter restaurants and shops, and use of soap in bathrooms, etc. but did you know that the word of God has that effect on our spiritual life? Ephesians 5:25-26 says, *"Husbands, love your wives, just as Christ loved the church and gave himself up for her to make her holy, cleansing her by the washing with water through the word, and to present her to himself as a radiant church, without stain or wrinkle or any other blemish, but holy and blameless."*

The Word of God has great power to purify your life. Jesus said to his disciples, *"You are already clean because of the word I have spoken to you."* The word has a cleansing effect. I can always tell when a person has stopped reading their Bible just by the things they say and do. It doesn't take long before their love for Jesus has grown cold and sin starts running rampant in their lives.

I don't know about you, but when I pick up the Word of God and read it, I find myself repenting of all sorts of things. I read a passage and I'm like, "Oh Lord, I have not been doing that, I'm sorry," or "Holy Spirit, I did that same thing again today and I have grieved you. I am so sorry." My reading of the Word is one long confession session…lol. But He has already forgiven me, praise God. It was done on the cross 2000 years ago, and there is no more sacrifice to be made. I am just acknowledging where I have missed it and coming back into alignment with His Word and His will for my life. Repentance means to turn around; to go a different way. It is submitting our will to His.

"The Word of God is alive and active. Sharper than any double-edged sword, it penetrates even to dividing soul and spirit, joints and marrow; it judges the thoughts and attitudes of the heart" (Hebrews 4:12).

As I read the Word, the Holy Spirit reveals my heart to me, and I can see exactly where I need to change. How many times have you read the Word of God and felt convicted about something? That is the Holy Spirit using the sword to cut to the quick as they say. We need God's Word to cut off the rubbish in our lives and to change us into His image.

In a Covid world, we wash frequently. If you never came in contact with soap, you would remain dirty. In the same way, we need a good wash in the Word. If you never come in contact with the living, powerful Word of God, then you will never get the pollution of this world off your life.

Blessings my friend, have a wonderful day.

Day 24

ood morning, my friend,

When my children were young, I took them to a large public swimming pool for an outing. As they played in the pool, I sat on the grass watching them. I could see many other mothers sitting around the edge of the pool doing the same thing. Suddenly, a child's voice rang out high pitched and urgent, "Mummy!!" It was a cry for help, and every single mother sitting around that pool went into high alert. Was that our child calling? All heads faced the same direction, and we were all looking intently to see if it was one of ours. Shortly, we could see a mother running towards the pool, so everyone settled back and breathed a sigh of relief. Since then, I have thought many times about that cry and the immediate response it got, and it makes me think about my Heavenly Father and just how much He cares for us. Would he react differently if he heard his child cry out? Psalm 34:17 says, *"The righteous cry out, and the Lord hears them; he delivers them from ALL their troubles."*

I looked up the meaning of those words in the Hebrew text. When it says, 'cry out', it means 'to shriek.' I remembered that child's shriek in the pool and the immediate response of the mother. The words 'from all our troubles' literally mean – the whole, all, any, every. I think that pretty much covers it. We have a Father in Heaven who is watching over us and has promised to deliver us from ALL our troubles when we cry out, and just in case you don't think that your Heavenly Father sees you, here are some verses to reassure you that you ARE being watched.

Psalm 121:8:

"The Lord will watch over your coming and going, both now and forevermore."

Psalm 32:8:

"I will instruct you and teach you in the way you should go; I will counsel you with my loving eye on you."

1 Peter 3:12:

"For the eyes of the Lord are toward the righteous, and his ears attend to their prayer, but the face of the Lord is against those who do evil."

So, whatever your need is today, cry out to your Heavenly Father. Call for his help like a little child. Believe that He sees you, hears you, and is delivering you out of ALL your troubles. We have his promise.

Be blessed, my friend. Have a wonderful day.

Day 25

Good morning, my friend,

I love the passage of scripture in Philippians 1:6, which says, *"Being confident of this, that he who began a good work in you will carry it on to completion until the day of Christ Jesus."*

There is something so reassuring about that verse. Isn't it good to know that the Master Craftsman is molding us into his own image? He hasn't finished yet and will continue his work on us right up until He returns. We are His masterpiece!

Psalm 138:8 says, *"The Lord will vindicate me; your love, Lord, endures forever— do not abandon the works of your hands."*

Hebrews 12:2:

"Looking unto Jesus, the author and finisher of our faith, who for the joy that was set before him endured the cross, despising the shame, and is set down at the right hand of the throne of God" (NKJV)

Ephesians 2:10:

"For we are God's handiwork, created in Christ Jesus to do good works, which God prepared in advance for us to do."

Psalm 139:13:

"For you created my innermost being; you knit me together in my mother's womb. I praise you because I am fearfully and wonderfully made; your works are wonderful….Your eyes saw my unformed body; all the days ordained for me were written

in your book before one of them came to be."

God has a divine plan for our lives; He has the blueprint, so to speak. All we need to do is submit to his plan, and the more we submit ourselves to Him, the more we will become like Him. It is a case of yielding to the hand of the Potter and allowing him to bring us to perfection.

We are all on a journey together. Some of us are further along the road than others, but we are all going to make it! He is going to complete what he has started in us. We have His word on it!

Blessings in abundance, have a wonderful day.

Day 26

Good morning, my friend,

David was hiding in a cave when he wrote the following Psalm, so he knew what it was like to endure persecution and affliction. He had nowhere else to turn but God. Psalm 34:1, *"The LORD is near to the broken-hearted; He saves the contrite in spirit. Many are the afflictions of the righteous, but the LORD delivers him from them all."*

That word 'deliver' in Hebrew means 'snatches away' and 'rescues.' The meaning of the word 'afflictions' is 'evil things'. When we are enduring hardship, persecution, and perplexing circumstances, we cry out to the Lord. He has promised to deliver us. In fact, his name is Deliverer – Romans 11:26. In the Old Testament, the word 'deliver' has two meanings - 'natan' is used over 1,200 times. It means to deliver from the power of others, usually their enemies. The other word 'nasal' means to snatch away, draw out, which focuses on God's removal of those who are going through trouble or danger. In the New Testament, the word 'deliver' has several meanings, two of which are 'rhuoma', which means to rescue or deliver from danger or distress, and 'exaireo', meaning to take out of. Believers are to pray for deliverance from the threat of evil that dominates the world (Matt 6:13; Luke 11:4) and by God's power, believers are delivered from 'this present evil age' (Galatians 1:4) and the power of Satan's reign (Colossians 1:13). The ultimate deliverance will be when Jesus comes again (Romans 11:26 and 1 Thessalonians 1:10)[6]

When we were travelling in Israel, the Lord sent an angel to deliver us. We were in a dangerous place, not knowing what to do, on a lonely stretch of road in the pitch black during a bad storm, when a man came over to us from a car that was parked in the bushes. He leaned into our car window and said, "I've been sitting here waiting for you to come. Follow me, and I will get you out of here." We had never seen him before, but we were able to follow him out of the dangerous place we were in to safety. He waved us on, and then seemed to disappear because we couldn't see where he went. You may not be in a dangerous place, but you may be enduring distress, persecution or affliction. God has promised to deliver you.

Paul the Apostle went through way more than most of us would even imagine or think, and yet he said, *"My persecutions, and the sufferings that came upon me in Antioch, Iconium, and Lystra. What persecutions I endured! Yet the Lord rescued me from all of them"* (2 Timothy 3:11).

Jesus is our Deliverer!

Be blessed and have a wonderful day.

---

[6] William E. Brown, "Deliver," in *Baker's Evangelical Dictionary of Biblical Theology*, ed. Walter A. Elwell (Grand Rapids: Baker Books, 1996).

Day 27

Good morning, my friend,

As I waited on the Lord for a Word for you, I heard the scripture verse *"For from Him, and through Him, and to Him, are all things"* (Romans 11:36). Twice the Lord brought the same verse to my mind during the day, so I believe God wants to say something about it.

We came from Him, made in His image. That is why Satan was so envious of our position and standing in God, and that is why he tempted Adam and Eve to give away their rule and sovereignty on the earth. He was just a created being, but we came from God (Ecclesiastes 12:7). Our spirit came out of the Father and was sent to the earth to put on flesh and be knit together in our mother's womb. We are sons and daughters of the Living God. We came with a destiny in God to fulfill and even the number of our days was recorded in our book in Heaven. We were chosen in Him even before the foundation of the earth. That by itself should make you sing and dance! But when Adam sinned, that life-connection to the Living God was broken. Jesus came to redeem mankind and reconcile us to God. When we accept His great salvation, we are brought back into right relationship with Him.

Everything we do should be through Him. Jesus is the head, and we are his body. We are just an extension of Him on this earth. In Romans 8:37 we read, *"No, in all these things we are more than conquerors through him who loved us."*

"I have been crucified with Christ, and I no longer live, but Christ lives in me. The life I live in the body, I live by faith in the Son of God, who loved me and gave Himself up for me" (Galatians 2:20, BSB). The whole of the Godhead bodily dwells in us. He is our source of supply. He is the vine, and we are the branches. Our life flows out from Him and without Him we can do nothing!

Jesus prayed, *"I am not asking on behalf of them alone, but also on behalf of those who will believe in Me through their message, that all of them may be one, as You, Father, are in Me, and I am in You. May they also be in Us, so that the world may believe that You sent Me. I have given them the glory You gave Me, so that they may be one as We are one"* (John 17:20, BSB).

We return our gratitude and praise to the Father. All honour, glory, power, might and dominion be His forever more! The Bible says that one day every knee will bow, and every tongue will acknowledge that Jesus Christ is Lord. Why don't we start today? Begin your day with worship and praise to God for who He is. He is Almighty God, Creator of the Universe, but He is also your Father. How amazing is that?

Have a wonderful day, my friend.

Day 28

Good morning, my friend,

I have noticed that one of the biggest ploys of the enemy is to get us so distracted that we no longer have time for the Word of God or prayer. The devil doesn't mind if we are doing 'good things' just so long as we are not spending time in God's presence. I know that I must watch for this myself. I can be running around helping people, teaching, talking about the Lord with friends, watching Christian television, going to Church, reading good books, etc. etc. etc.....the list is endless, and they are all good things, but they crowd my life until one day, I realise that my life has become just a ritual of doing things for God, without the relationship. Like someone once said, "If God died, would most of us even know?"

Distractions are anything that takes our focus off what is important. Colossians 3:2 says, *"Set your mind on things above, not on earthly things."* And in Hebrews 12:1-2 it says, *"Therefore, since we are surrounded by such a great cloud of witnesses, let us throw off everything that hinders and the sin that so easily entangles. And let us run with perseverance the race marked out for us, fixing our eyes on Jesus, the pioneer and perfecter of faith. For the joy set before him, he endured the cross, scorning its shame, and sat down at the right hand of the throne of God."*

God wants our undivided attention. Time is short, and the days are evil. It is time not to let the distractions take us away from developing our relationship with Him.

Have a wonderful day my friend.

Day 29

Good morning, my friend,

Exodus 16:4, *"Then the Lord said to Moses, "I will rain down bread from heaven for you. The people are to go out each day and gather enough for that day."*

1 Corinthians 10:3-4, *"They all ate the same spiritual food and drank the same spiritual drink, for they drank from the spiritual rock that accompanied them, and that rock was Christ."*

Nehemiah 9:15, *"In their hunger You gave them bread from heaven; in their thirst You brought them water from the rock. You told them to go in and possess the land which You had sworn to give them."*

The story of Moses and the Children of Israel is an amazing story. I love to tell it to the children at school, and as I talk about how God led the Children of Israel out of Egypt, I see so many parallels to our Christian walk today. They left Egypt (the world), went through the Red Sea (baptism), they ate from the same spiritual food (the Word of God), and drank the water from the rock (the rock – Jesus, the water – the Holy Spirit). Notice in Nehemiah it says that God gave them the bread, and the water, then He told them to go in and possess the land which He had promised to give them. If we think we can go in to possess all that God has promised us, then we need to eat the bread and drink the water first. Without the Word of God and the Holy Spirit, you will never be able to possess all that God has promised you.

Every day is a new day in God. Each day has new challenges, new trials to face, new battles to fight, and new victories to be won. Each morning, God will give you exactly what you need for each day, so open the Word of God and feed on it. Drink deeply from the Holy Spirit, for it is He who will equip you, help you, guide you, strengthen you, comfort you, and give you courage. He will not give you courage today for what you will go through tomorrow, but He will give you what you need at the time you need it.

We are told not to worry about tomorrow, for tomorrow will worry about itself. (Matthew 6:34) Live each day on the spiritual food and drink that God gives you for that day. Smell the roses, listen to the birds, enjoy the sunshine, spend time in God's presence, drink of the Holy Spirit; and gather enough spiritual food from the word for your day.

Have a wonderful day. I love you all heaps.

Day 30

ood morning, my friend,

"Are you satisfied?" I was just going to sit down at my computer when I heard the Lord speak to my heart and it got me thinking. Am I satisfied with the status quo and happy to just plod along taking life as it comes, barely existing, putting up with sickness, weakness, and everything else that comes along, living life as if God never existed, or am I hungry and thirsty to really know Him and have an intimate relationship with Him? I remember an old song we used to sing that always stirred my heart when we sang it:

Springs of Living Water

I thirsted in the barren land of sin and shame,
And nothing satisfying there I found;
But to the blessed cross of Christ one day I came,
Where springs of living water did abound.

Chorus

Drinking at the springs of living water,
Happy now am I, my soul they satisfy;
Drinking at the springs of living water,
O wonderful and bountiful supply. [7]

God has so much more for us, but are we hungry and thirsty for Him or are we just content with how we are? Psalm 107:9 says, *"For He satisfies the thirsty and fills the hungry with good things."*

When we get hungry and thirsty and long for God, that is when we will truly be satisfied by Him and all that He is. David the Psalmist, was a man after God's own heart because he longed for God. He wrote in Psalm 63:1-5 while he was in the wilderness of Judah, *"You, God, are my God, earnestly I seek you; I thirst for you, my whole being longs for you, in a dry and parched land where there is no water. I have seen you in the sanctuary and beheld your power and your glory. Because your love is better than life, my lips will glorify you. I will praise you as long as I live, and in your name I will lift up my hands. I will be fully satisfied as with the richest of foods; with singing lips my mouth will praise you."* That's the type of hunger and thirst I am talking about.

I don't know about you, but it is often in the dry places, and in the tough times that we start to get hungry, thirsty and long for Him, but wouldn't it be better if we longed for Him all the time? Maybe we wouldn't go through some of the 'stuff' we go through if we did. God has promised to satisfy us when we seek for Him with our whole heart. (Jeremiah 29:13).

Be blessed my friend and have a wonderful day.

www.ingramcontent.com/pod-product-compliance
Lightning Source LLC
Chambersburg PA
CBHW061803050726
47598CB00002B/851